LITTLE HISTORIES

Viking Times

Christopher Maynard

Kingfisher

Contents

Viking raiders

Although they never ruled over vast areas of land, the Vikings became famous far and wide as fierce and bloodthirsty raiders. All over Europe, in the years 800 to 1100, fleets of Viking ships sailed along coasts and up rivers, to attack towns and monasteries and steal their treasure.

Viking explorers

The Vikings were more than just raiders. They were also farmers, traders, craftworkers, and above all brave explorers and settlers. Their homelands were in northern Europe, in the countries that are now Scandinavia.

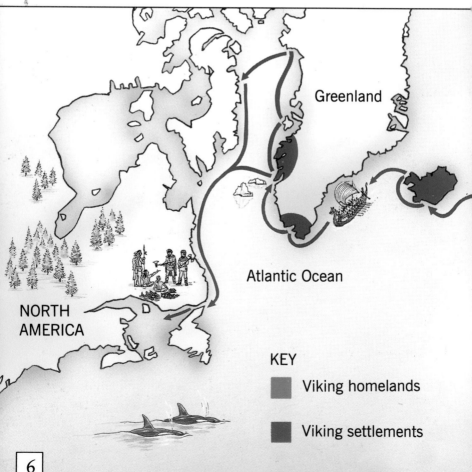

Greenland

Atlantic Ocean

NORTH AMERICA

KEY

Viking homelands

Viking settlements

There is little good farming land in Scandinavia, and it was difficult for the Vikings to grow enough food – one reason why they turned to the sea. They sailed south all the way to Italy and west to North America. They rowed down the rivers of eastern Europe and traded in Russia and Arabia.

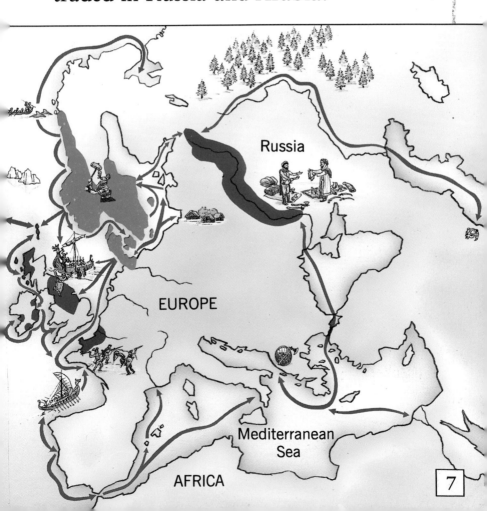

Russia

EUROPE

Mediterranean
Sea

AFRICA

Ships and sailors

The Vikings were able to reach new lands and settle in them because they were superb shipbuilders and sailors. Longships were used for war. For trade, and to carry settlers and all their animals and goods to new lands, wider ships called knorrs were built.

GETTING THERE

The Vikings didn't have compasses, let alone any of the other equipment that sailors now use to help them find their way. Whenever they could, Viking sailors hugged the coastline and watched out for familiar landmarks. In open seas, they used weather vanes to tell which direction the wind was coming from, and steered by the stars and the Sun.

Living on a farm

On most Viking farms, everyone lived in one big building called a longhouse. All around it were sheds for animals, workshops and storing things.

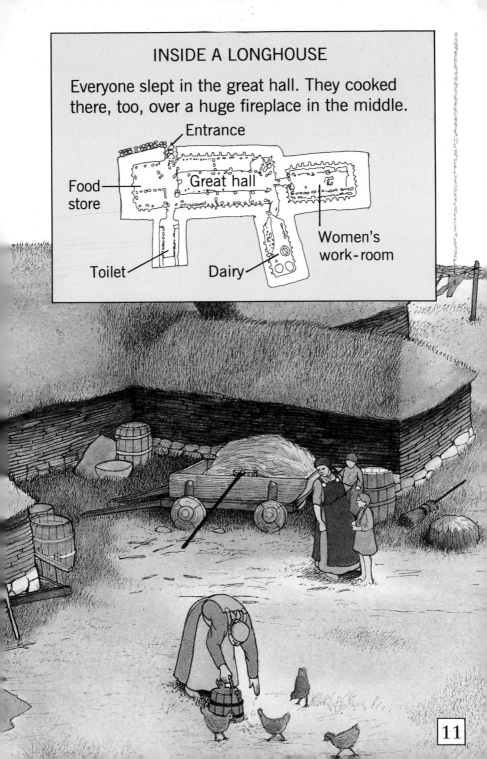

INSIDE A LONGHOUSE

Everyone slept in the great hall. They cooked there, too, over a huge fireplace in the middle.

Entrance

Food store

Great hall

Women's work-room

Toilet

Dairy

A busy household

I n winter, farms in Scandinavia were often snowed in. There was little farm work to do outside, so the great hall bustled with life.

The women spun wool and flax into yarn, then wove it into cloth on big upright looms. With enough food stored to last them through the winter, the men had time to repair tools and carve wood.

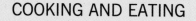

COOKING AND EATING

Food was stewed in a big iron pot, roasted on a spit over the fire, or baked in a pit below it. Porridge was a favourite meal, as was a bubbling meat and vegetable stew. The Vikings drank beer and wine, and made a drink called mead from honey.

Clothes and jewellery

Viking women wore a long linen or woollen dress. Over the top went a tunic held in place by shoulder straps and big brooches. Men wore woollen trousers, and a long-sleeved linen shirt under a tunic and a cloak.

Married women wore a linen headdress. Men had tight wool or leather caps.

Men's cloaks were fastened at the right shoulder to leave the sword arm free.

Men and women liked to wear jewellery.

Leather shoes were made waterproof with grease.

MAKE VIKING JEWELLERY

Women used big brooches to fasten the straps of their tunics. Sometimes a necklace was strung between them.

To make your own, you'll need stiff card, scissors, glue, beads, kitchen foil, needle and thread, tape and two big safety pins.

1 Cut two big circles out of card.

2 Glue a few beads to one side of both cards. Let them dry.

3 Coat the beads and cards with glue, then smooth over some foil. Rub the foil gently around the beads to make them stand out.

4 Cut a 30-cm length of cotton and thread the needle.

5 Push the needle through the bottom of a brooch. Pull the cotton through and tie off the end.

6 Thread on beads until there's about 6 cm cotton left. Sew it through the other brooch and tie it off.

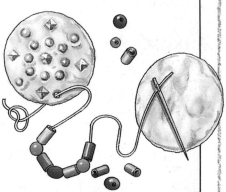

7 Glue and tape a safety pin to the back of each brooch.

A Viking town

Not all Vikings stayed on farms. Some lived in small market towns. Bustling Hedeby, in Denmark, was known far and wide for the wealth and skill of its merchants and craftworkers.

KEY TO TOWN

① House walls were built from willow twigs woven through sturdy wooden posts.
② Roofs were thatched with rushes.
③ Main streets were paved with logs.
④ Women did their washing in the stream.
⑤ A high, earth wall protected the town.
⑥ Tunnel-gates let people in and out.
⑦ Cargo ships tied up at the dock.

17

Sword makers

Although they fought with axes, spears, and bows and arrows, the Vikings' favourite weapon was a sword. A really well-made sword was often passed down from father to son.

Swords were made in a forge. First the blade was hammered from twisted rods of red-hot iron. Then a beautiful hilt, or handle, was decorated with strips of gold and silver.

MAKE A VIKING SWORD

The Vikings were so proud of their swords they often gave them names, like Leg-biter.

You'll need some wallpaper paste, rubber gloves, stiff card, scissors, old newspapers, paintbrushes, gold paint and clear varnish.

1 Mix up a bowl of wallpaper paste.

2 Cut a sword shape from card, and tear about eight pages of paper into small strips as long as your hand.

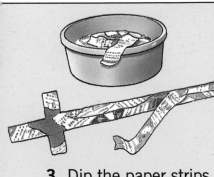

4 Paint your sword gold. Write a name on it when the paint is dry, then seal it all with a coat of varnish.

3 Dip the paper strips in the wallpaper paste and smooth them on the card. Cover the sword, then let it dry. Add two more layers of paper in the same way.

Keeping the law

Vikings settled arguments about land ownership and crimes such as stealing at special outdoor meetings called Things. Each local area held its own. In later years, Things were also held for whole countries.

Each Thing had its own set of laws. Only free men could vote, but they often took their families along with them. A Thing was a great place to hear the latest news and gossip, and to arrange marriages.

Stories and poems

The Viking alphabet was made up of letters called runes, and people wrote by carving runes into wood or stone. Even a short message took a long time to carve, so stories and poems were mostly learned by heart.

People would travel a long way to listen to storytellers. Favourite tales were about the battles and adventures of great kings and warriors, or the many Viking gods.

CARVE A VIKING NAME PLATE

You'll need a mixing bowl, rolling pin, some plastic film, an oiled baking tray, a sharp pencil and some poster paints, as well as:

300 g plain flour
300 g salt
1 tbsp oil
200 ml water

1 Mix the flour, salt, oil and water into a dough and knead it until it's smooth.
2 Put the dough on to the plastic film and roll it out to about 1.5 cm thick.

3 Cut out an oval. Turn it on to the tray.

4 Peel off the film and make a hole on each side of the oval with the pencil. Now carve your initials using runes for the letters.

5 Ask a grown-up to bake it at gas mark 4 (180°C), until hard (about 10 minutes).
6 Let your name plate cool before you paint it brightly.

↑	ᛒ	ᚵ	ᛓ	ᛁ	ᛂ	ᚠ	ᚱ	ᛉ	ᛁ	ᚱ	ᛉ
A	B	C	D	E	F	G	H	IJ	K	L	M

ᚺ	ᚭ	K	ᚠ	ᚱ	ᛃ	ᛏ	ᛜ	ᛪ	ᛐ	ᛄ
N	O	P	Q	R	S	T	UVW	X	Y	Z

Viking longships

The Vikings wrote stories and poems about their longships, too, and gave them names like *Long Serpent* and *Wave Walker*. They carved beautiful decorations for them, as well.

Ships were usually built in winter, when little farm work could be done. They were made of oak wood, and built as close to the water as possible.

Once the ship's framework was in place, huge planks were fixed one above the other, overlapping a bit, to form its hull. To make the joins watertight, they were stuffed with animal hair dipped in sticky tar.

Make a longship

S ome longships were decorated with fierce animal heads, and warriors sometimes fixed their shields along the sides. Here's how to make a longship, with an animal head and Viking shields.

You'll need a small box (such as a shoebox), some kitchen foil and scissors, an empty matchbox, a drinking straw, some modelling clay, glue, two sheets of thin card, poster paints and some string.

1 Draw curves along each side of the box, then cut them out.

2 Put the box in the middle of a big sheet of foil and fold the foil in over the sides. Shape a foil figurehead at one end and a post at the other.

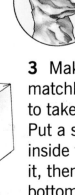

3 Make a hole in the matchbox, big enough to take the straw mast. Put a small lump of clay inside the box to weight it, then glue it into the bottom of your ship.

4 Cut a sail from some card. Make holes in it for the straw mast to fit through, then paint it.

5 Slip the straw mast through the sail, then glue the mast into the hole in the matchbox.

6 Tie string between the figurehead, mast and back post to keep the mast steady.

7 Cut some shields out of card and paint them. Glue them to the sides of your longship when they are completely dry. Now you're ready to sail your longship!

Ship of death

Many Vikings believed that after they died, their spirits sailed off to a new life with the gods. Important people such as chiefs or warriors were often buried in a ship, with their clothes, furniture and tools, as well as food for the journey. The ship was set on fire, too, sometimes.

VIKING GODS

The Vikings believed in many gods and goddesses. The greatest was Odin the god of the de He had an eight-legged horse an two pet ravens. Each night the reported to him that had happ in the world th .

Glossary

cargo – goods carried by a boat

flax – a plant whose stringy stem is used to make cloth

forge – the place where a blacksmith works

homeland – the place where a people originally come from

knorr – a Viking boat, built to carry animals, goods and people

longhouse – a Viking farmhouse

longship – a Viking warship

merchant – someone who buys and sells goods

monastery – a building where religious men, called monks, live and work

raider – someone who suddenly attacks a place, taking it by surprise

rune – a letter in the Viking alphabet

Scandinavia – part of northern Europe that includes Denmark, Norway and Sweden

settler – someone who comes to live in a new place

Thing – a meeting to settle an argument or pass laws

trade – the exchange of goods between peoples and countries to make money

Index

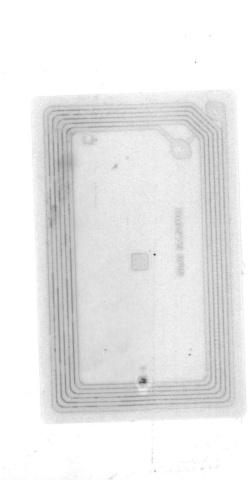